It's Nice to Know Someone Like You

Other books by

Blue Mountain Press INC

Come Into the Mountains, Dear Friend
by Susan Polis Schutz
I Want to Laugh, I Want to Cry
by Susan Polis Schutz
Peace Flows from the Sky
by Susan Polis Schutz
Someone Else to Love
by Susan Polis Schutz
I'm Not That Kind of Girl
by Susan Polis Schutz
Yours If You Ask
by Susan Polis Schutz
Love, Live and Share
by Susan Polis Schutz
The Language of Friendship
The Language of Love
The Language of Happiness
The Desiderata of Happiness
by Max Ehrmann
I Care About Your Happiness
by Kahlil Gibran/Mary Haskell
I Wish You Good Spaces
Gordon Lightfoot
We Are All Children Searching for Love
by Leonard Nimoy
Come Be with Me
by Leonard Nimoy
These Words Are for You
by Leonard Nimoy
Creeds to Love and Live By
On the Wings of Friendship
You've Got a Friend
Carole King
With You There and Me Here
The Dawn of Friendship
Once Only
by jonivan
Expressing Our Love
Just the Way I Am
Dolly Parton
You and Me Against the World
Paul Williams
Words of Wisdom, Words of Praise
Reach Out for Your Dreams
I Promise You My Love
Thank You for Being My Parents
A Mother's Love
A Friend Forever
gentle freedom, gentle courage
diane westlake
You Are Always My Friend
When We Are Apart
It Isn't Always Easy
My Sister, My Friend
Find Happiness In Everything You Do
by Susan Polis Schutz

It's Nice to Know Someone Like You

a collection of poems
by Peter A. McWilliams

Blue Mountain Press
Boulder, Colorado

Copyright © Blue Mountain Arts, Inc., 1981.
Copyright © Peter A. McWilliams, 1981.
All rights reserved, including the right to
reproduce this book or portions thereof in any form.

Library of Congress Number: 81-68587
ISBN: 0-88396-151-2

Manufactured in the United States of America

First Printing: October, 1981
Second Printing: February, 1982
Third Printing: April, 1982
Fourth Printing: September, 1982

Acknowledgments: Thanks to the Blue Mountain Arts creative staff, with special thanks to Douglas Pagels.
Additional acknowledgments are listed on page 64.

Blue Mountain Press INC

P.O. Box 4549, Boulder, Colorado 80306

Photo by Betty Bennett

Introduction

For this latest Blue Mountain Arts collection of my verse, I was asked to "write a little something . . . something as short as 'Love & Light'—as you always say—or as long as a page."

Well, my poems are short but my prose tends to ramble. "Love & Light" certainly sums it up as far as I'm concerned. (One of my favorite teachers on this planet, John-Roger, defines L.I.G.H.T. as "Living In God's Holy Thoughts;" and Love, well, we all know what Love is.)

But if I were to expand these two words to fill a page, how would I do it? I thought and thought and finally remembered something. (All writing seems to be remembering anyway: "Original" writing is simply remembering something that hasn't been written down before.) The "something" I remembered was a workshop I took called INSIGHT, and the parts I remembered were the only three ground rules for that workshop. They were:

—Take care of yourself so that you can help take care of others.
—Don't hurt yourself and don't hurt others.
—Use everything to your advantage.

As time has gone on, I have discovered that these three ground rules apply equally well in the life that exists beyond the five days of that workshop. In fact, I find that as I live my life more and more by these "rules," more and more I am filled with (as I always say . . .)

Love & Light

Peter

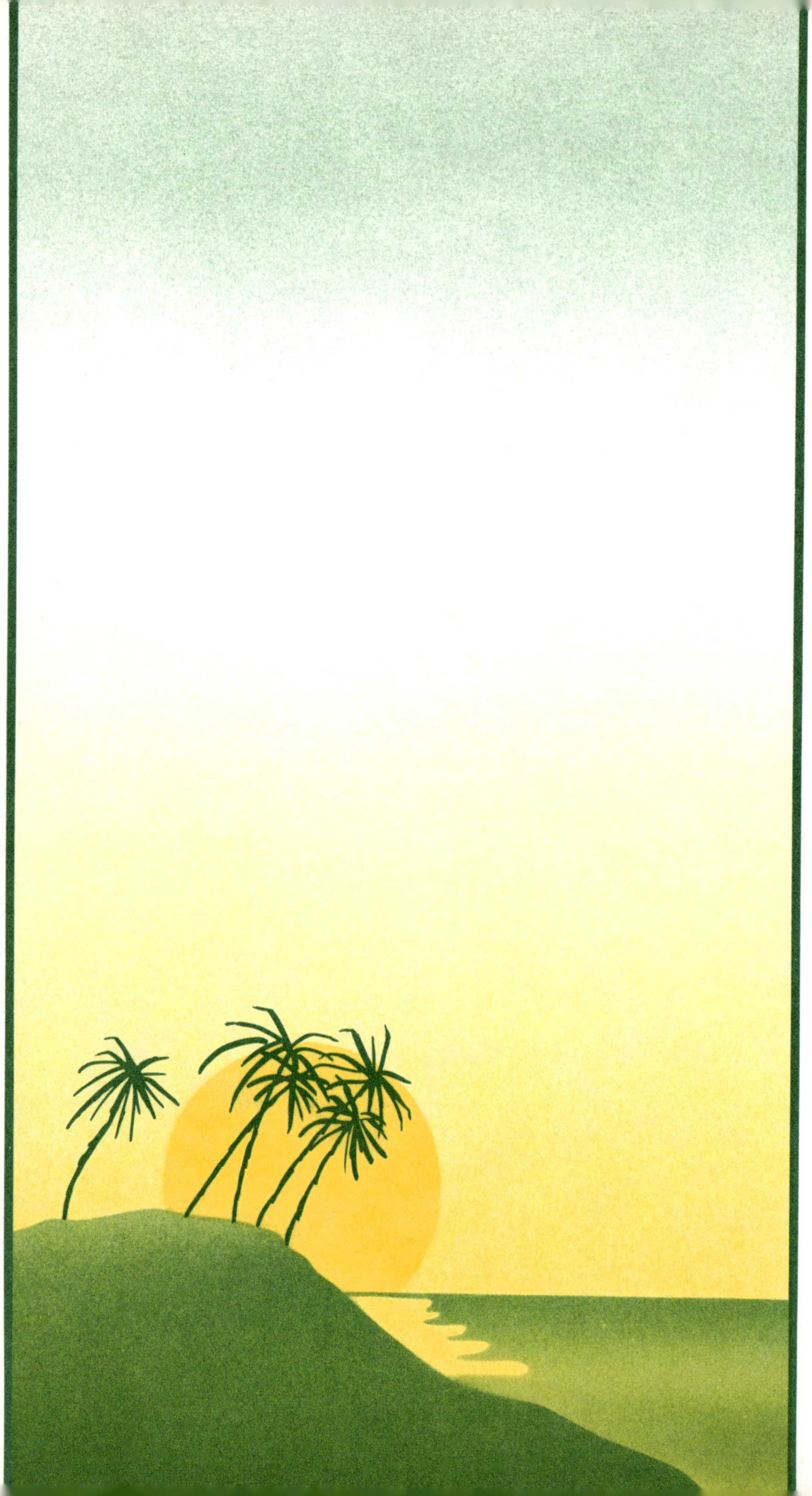

*You are a wonderful,
  worthy and loveable person.
Appreciate that
about yourself.
No one has ever been,
or will ever be,
quite like you.
You are an individual,
  an original,
and all those things that make you
uniquely you
are deserving of love
    and praise.*

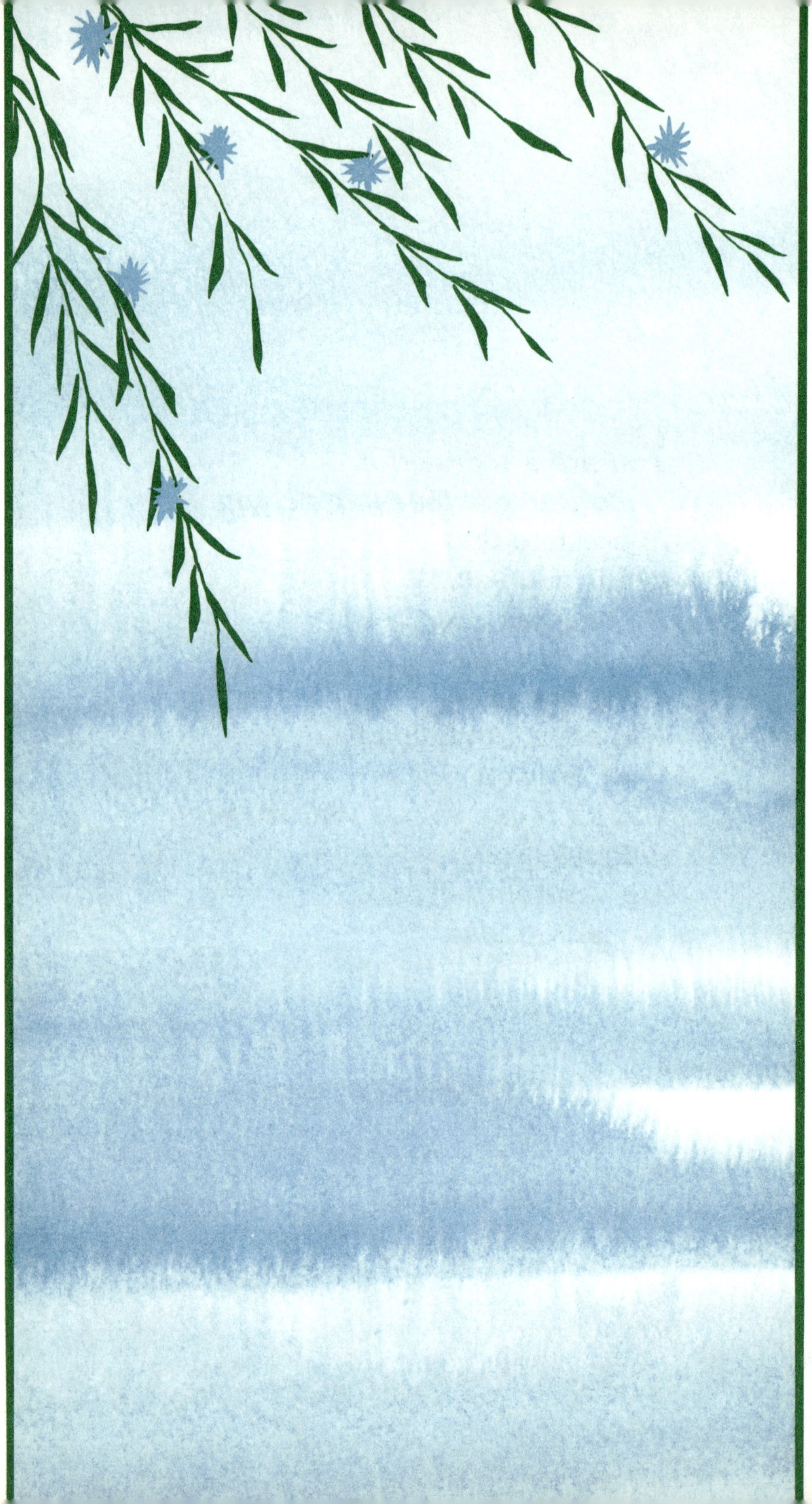

*It's so nice . . .
to have someone
to think about
and care about,
and to have
someone to plan with.
It's nice to have
someone who
really makes
a difference.
It's nice to have
someone to love.*

You
*are the nicest
thing I could
ever do for
myself.*

*I have
no thing
to share
with you
but my
 life.*

*I have
no thing
to experience
with you
but our
 love.*

this is all.

is all enough?

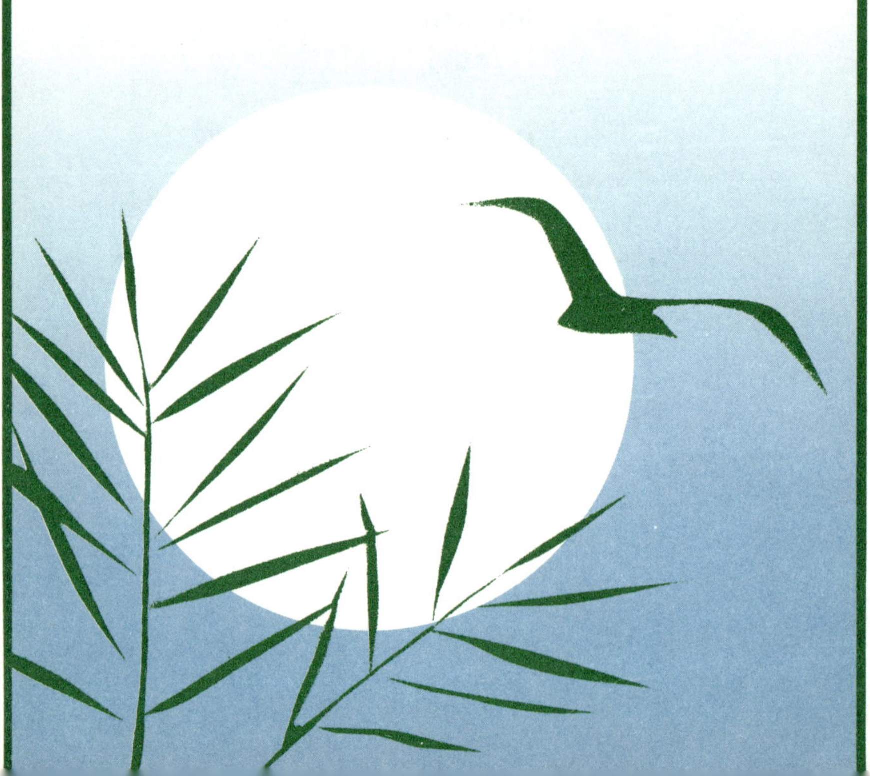

I love you
for the love you give me.

You love me
for the love I give you.

I do not know who first gave
or who first took
or where it all began

But I am happy that it did.

I am happy that it is.

I am happy as it is.

I am in short
  in long
  in love
    (and happy!)

You are worthy of the best.
And the best includes
a sense of inner happiness, and
people to share that
    happiness with.

You don't have to do
   anything special
   or be anyone special,
you just have to be . . .
amazing, wonderful you.

Come,
be with me.
together we'll discover
the secret spaces of the gods.

I would like to
know you.
Know you well.

your concepts . . .
where they came from.
where they are taking you.

what it is
that makes
you . . . you.

*I find many things
to be grateful for.*

*I say "thank you" for
warm mornings . . .
and all the love
you have ever offered.*

*I say "thank you" for
being there,
willing to be shared.*

A goal:

*To be
closer to God.*

*To be
closer to ourselves.*

*To be
closer to each other.*

*Togetherness
is not an end in itself
but a beginning.*

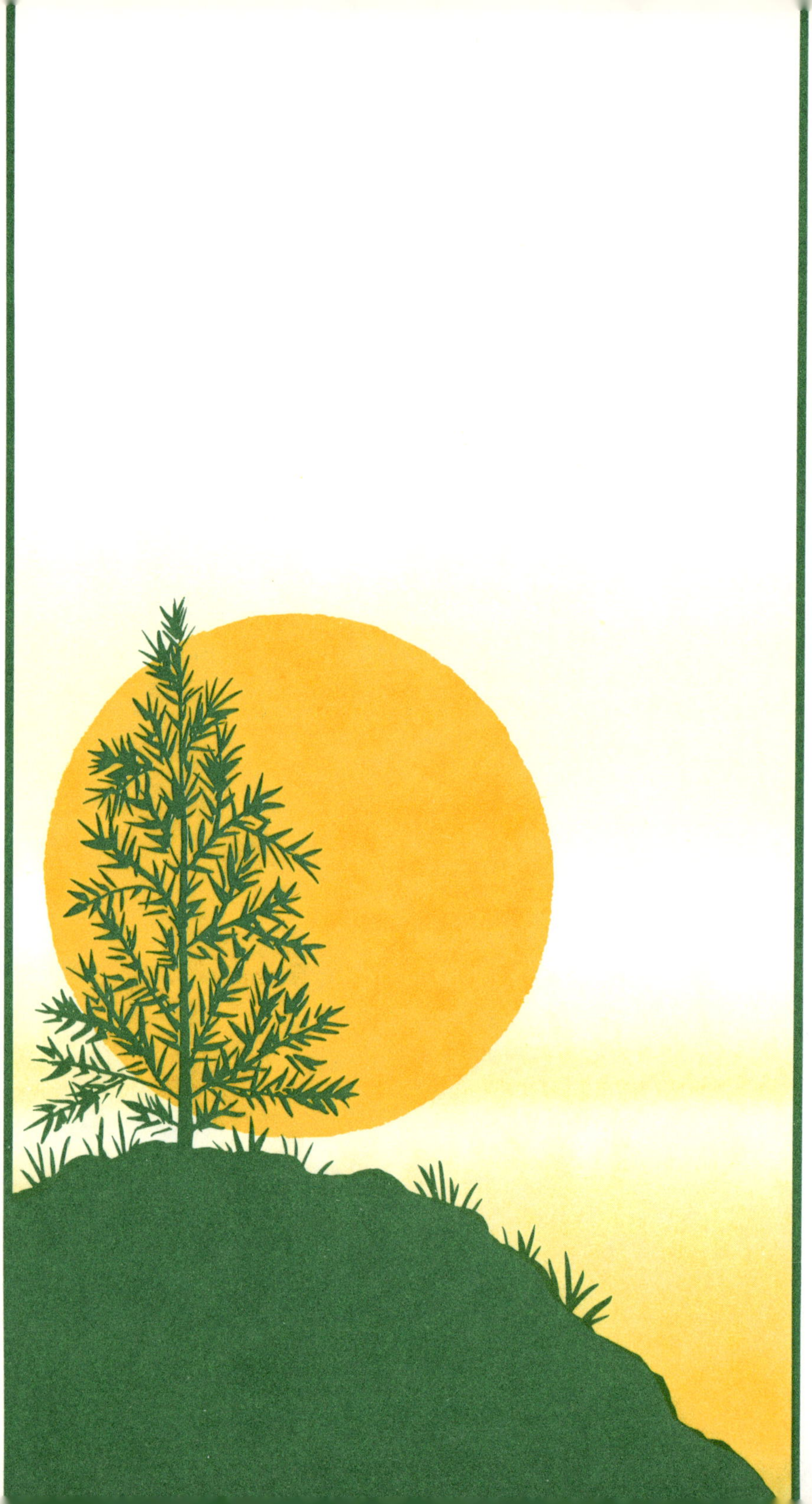

We must remember
that no one person
can make another person
  whole
or entire,
or entirely happy
forever after.
We must each find
our own personal basis
for completeness.

Once we realize this,
we can foster a relationship
that is based
not on unrealistic expectations
that may never be fulfilled,
but on the things
that really matter . . .
  trust and honesty,
    openness and love.

*The greatest gift
is to fill a need
unnoticed.*

*In being loved
I am filled full.*

*In loving
I am fulfilled.*

*L*ove is the most
 fulfilling experience
 in the world.
It starts inside of us
 and continues outward
 to each other.
Take care
 and delight
in your ability to love
 and be loved.

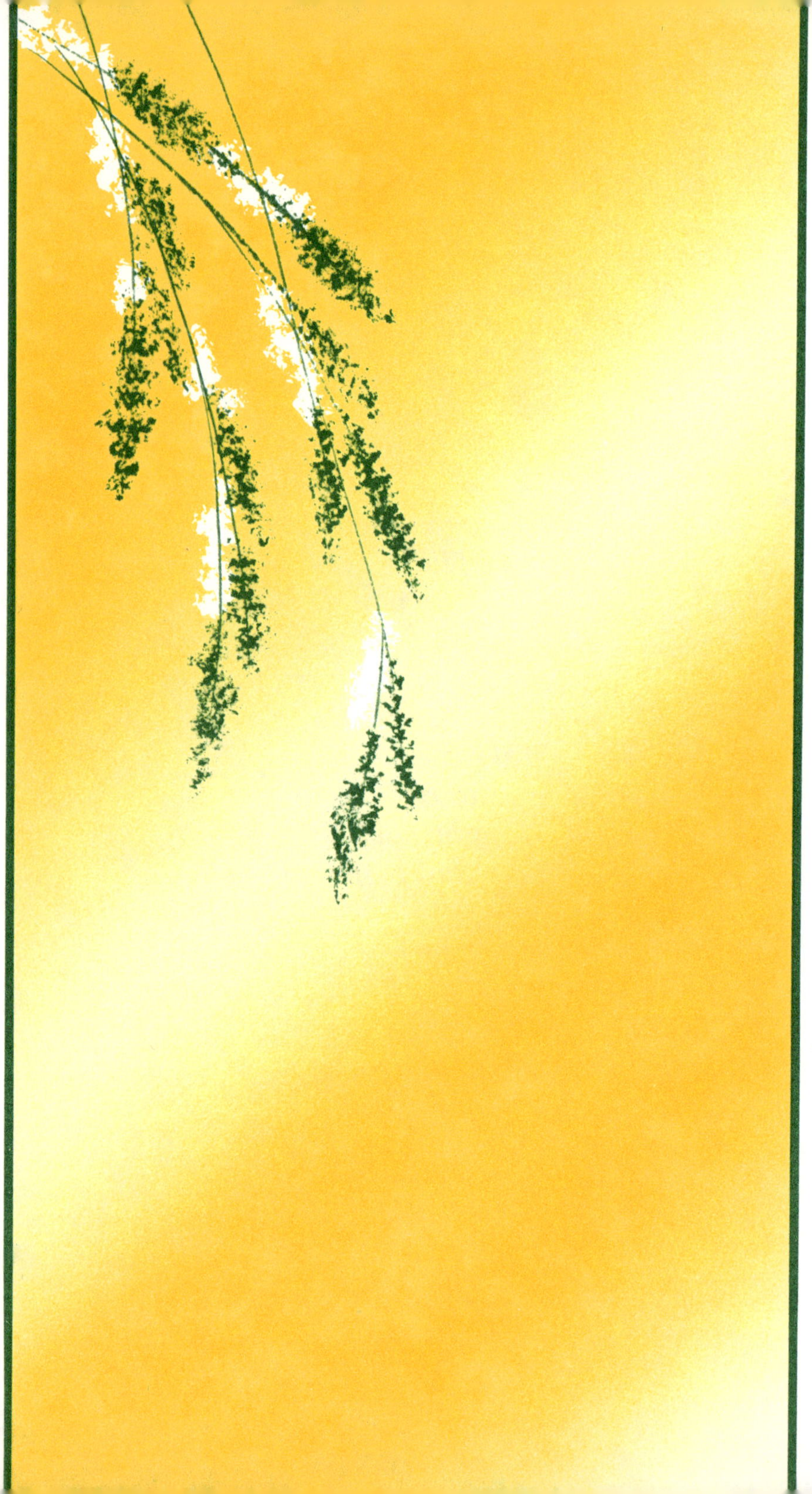

*if
you will
help me
find as
much
meaning
in my life
as I
have found
in our love,*

*I know
I shall
never
die*

Loving
is the most
creative force
of the universe.

Some times,
when only the Universe
is too vast for my
embrace,
 I think
 on you
 and smile.

*In those rare
moments when
all desires
have been fulfilled,*

*my mind
rests
on only
you.*

*This,
for me,
is Love.*

Love is

*knowing
&
growing
&
showing
&
sewing
&
hoeing
&
glowing
&
flowing
&
bestowing.*

love is two people rhyming.

*Instead of finding
"the right somebody to love,"
why not find the
loving
that's already inside
you?*

*Experience that loving.
Enjoy it.
Let it grow.*

*Then you're a loving person,
A living poem.*

*All you have to find then
is another "loving person."*

*This may be just as difficult as
finding "the right somebody to love,"
but the looking is likely to be
a lot more enjoyable.*

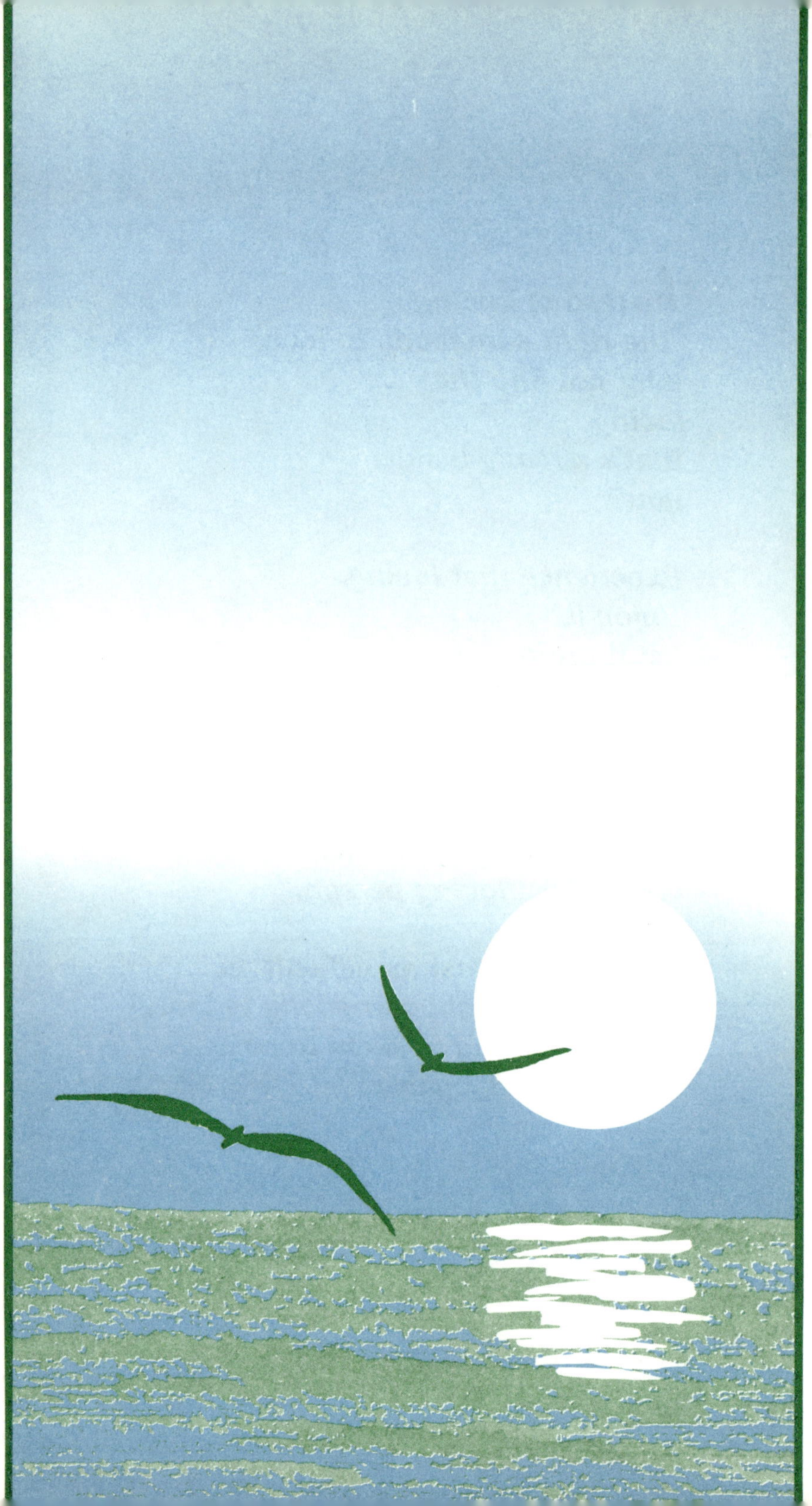

*The garden loves the rain
and, yes, this is love.*

*But the love I want for you
the love I want to give you
is the love
the rain
gives
the garden.*

Loving is giving freedom.

*I have been
free
now for
quite some time.

free
from the idea
that I needed
any one
to share with me
the limits of my
existence.

but now
you've
come along,
and I find
the lack of
you
turns my
alone
moments into
lonely ones.*

*I remember thinking once
that it would be good
if you left because
then I could get some
Important Things
done.*

*since you've left I've done
nothing. nothing
is as important
as you.*

Everything that reminds me of you gives me pleasure.

Everything reminds me of you.

*I don't need some
one
to be my joy.

I do need
someone
to share
my joys with.*

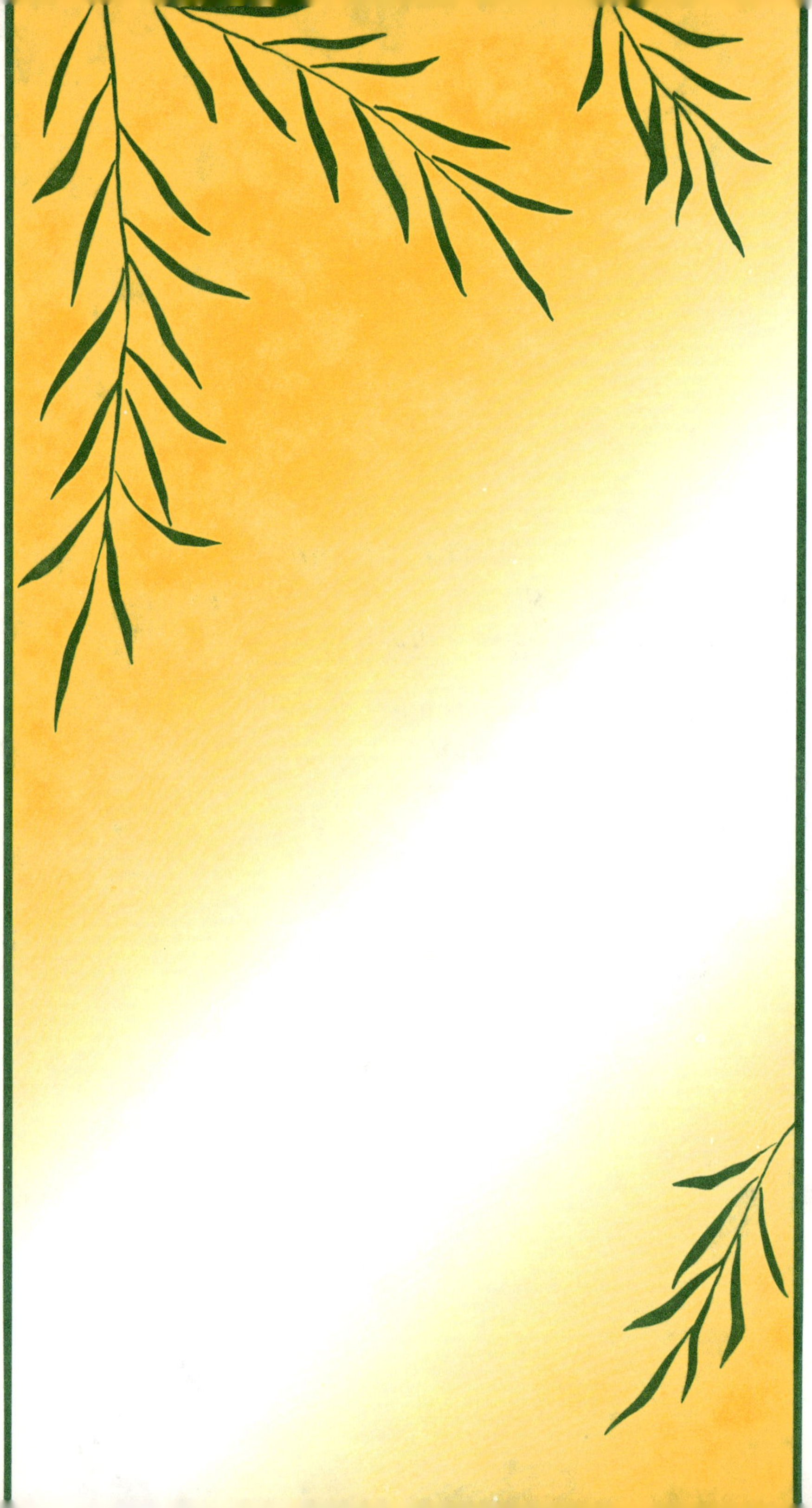

The world holds many wonders.

You are one of them.

Fascinating things are happening:
  good things
  bad things
  happy things
  sad things.
All are fascinating.

For you are in my world.

Sometimes
it all seems to fit.

In those moments
I appreciate you
most of all.

As I need you less
I love you more.

*I want
the feeling
I have
when I'm
near you
to be
with you
all the time.*

*Our life will be
more satisfying and enjoyable
if we seek out its richness,
appreciating every varied
and remarkable moment.
Our fulfillment of life
depends on our ability
to fully appreciate
    the present.*

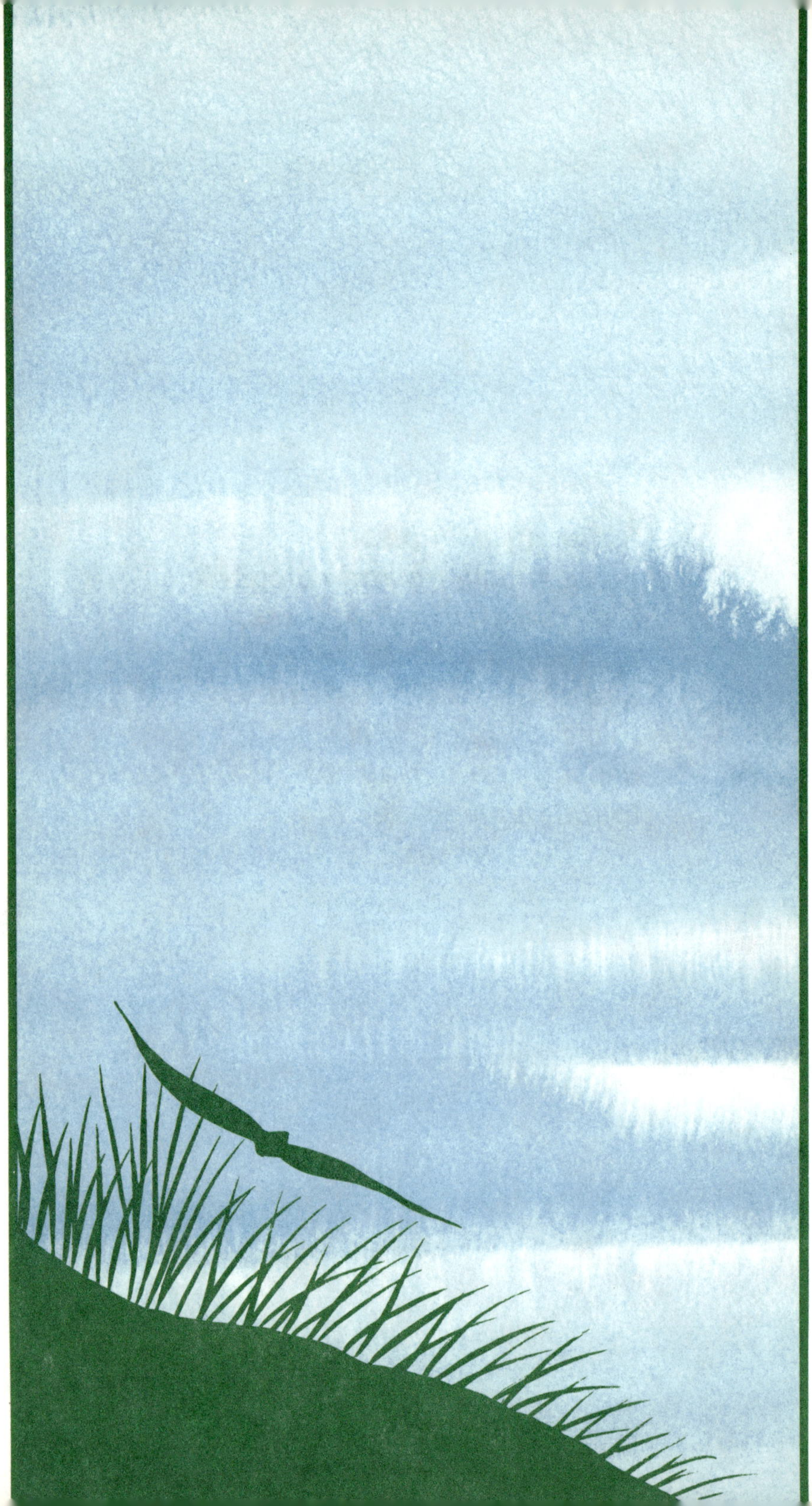

*Live your life as you wish
   it to be.
Make your life full
and rich
and vibrant
right now.*

*Don't store away
moments of pleasure
in your hope chest . . .
live them, enjoy them, now.*

*I will enjoy
your
smile
  &
    touch
     &
        words
       &
          love.*

*The difference between
  love
  and
  loving*

*is the difference between
  fish
  and
  fishing.*

*When I am with you
   I am transformed.
I feel transported
   to a magical land
of happiness
   and laughter
      and sunshine.

Toto, I don't
believe we're
in Kansas anymore.*

Growing...

*It is a funny thing about growth...
it has a ripple effect.
You may be surprised
at the number of rings that can
emanate from your growing process
in relating to other people.
First, you expand your horizons
by strengthening your self-image.
You receive a practical and
  psychological education.
Then you expand your inner horizons
  even more...*

*As others sense that you are
a changing, growing person,
you are more likely
to expand your circle of friends.*

*And somewhere . . .
on one of the rings that
results from your growth,
is someone to love . . .
someone with whom
to form a deep
and special relationship.
Growing . . . changing . . . appreciating.
It's all a circle, interdependent,
as inseparable as night from day.
Each part is important
to that remarkable thing
     called life.*

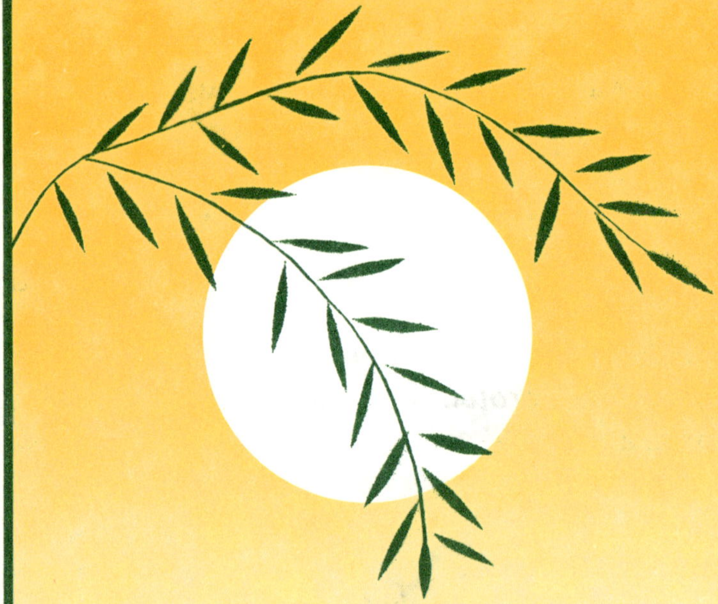

*For years
I wandered about life,
looking for some stabilizing force,
a constant that,
once found,
would bring peace
   security
      and happiness.
I sought this consistency
in many ways without luck.
Eventually I realized
that if it were "mine"
I would have to
look for it within myself.*

*I have a feeling that
maybe—just maybe*

*the search is over
& the journey has begun,*

maybe—just maybe.

Colors are brighter
since you've come to
stay a while.

my heart beats in time
with the universal
song of love.

loneliness . . . pain . . .
where are you hiding,
my long time comrades?

maybe they have gone
where you came from

God
created
all things,

but He took
special care
in crafting
the rose
and you.

*You make
    flowers
of my
hours.*

*today
was a
bouquet.*

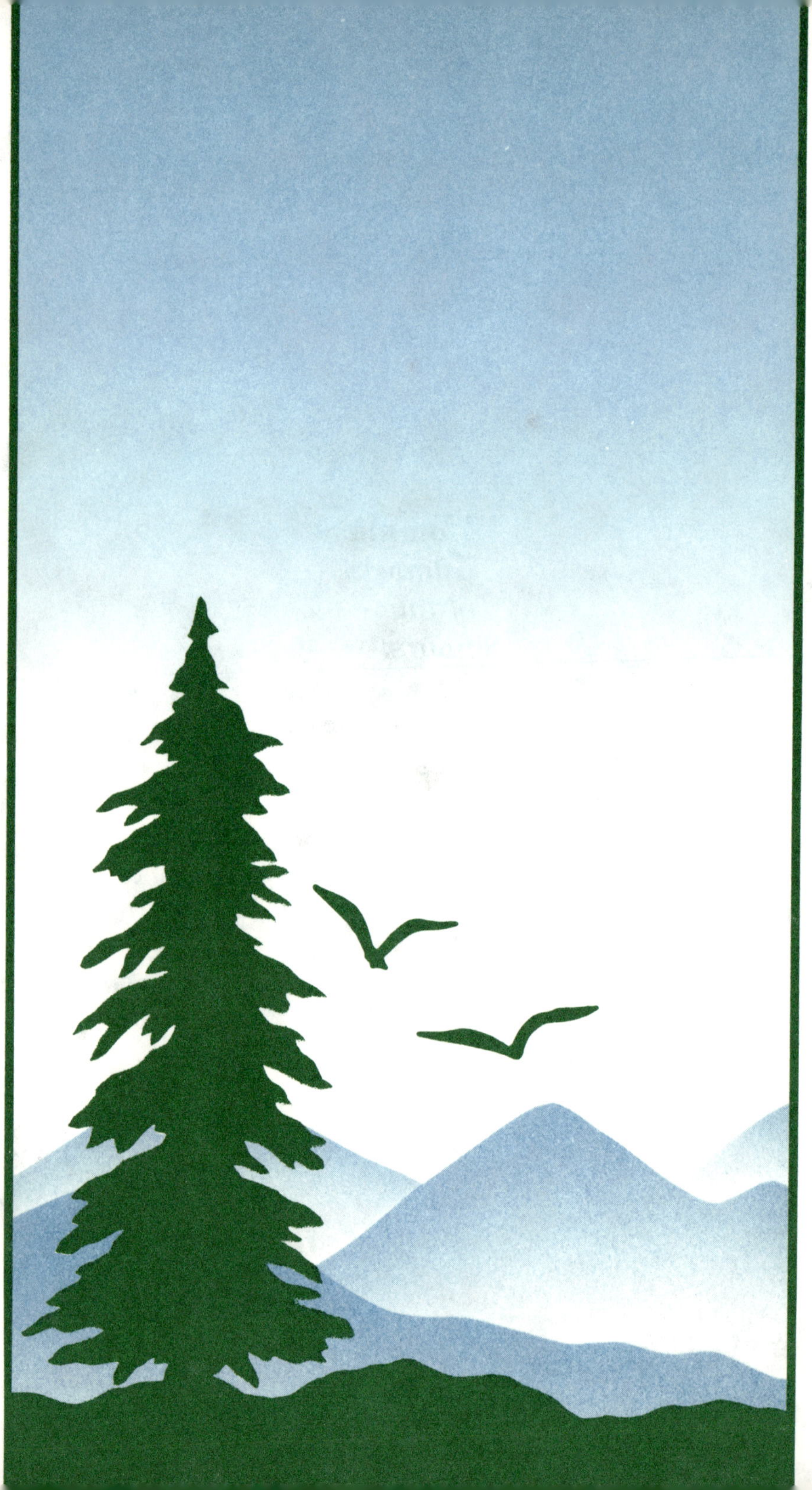

*Within me,
  you inspire
    desire,
      contemplation
      & creation.*

*Is this because I
love you,
or do I love you
because of this?*

Did I tell you
that I love you?

Maybe I was
too busy
loving
to tell.

But I do.
Oh yes, I do.

*Is it all right
if I daydream
aloud about us
with you?*

*In the space
between the words
is the place
where love lives*

*how do I count on thee?
let me love the ways.*

*When there are
joys
I want you for
sharing.
When there are
sorrows
I want you for
comfort.*

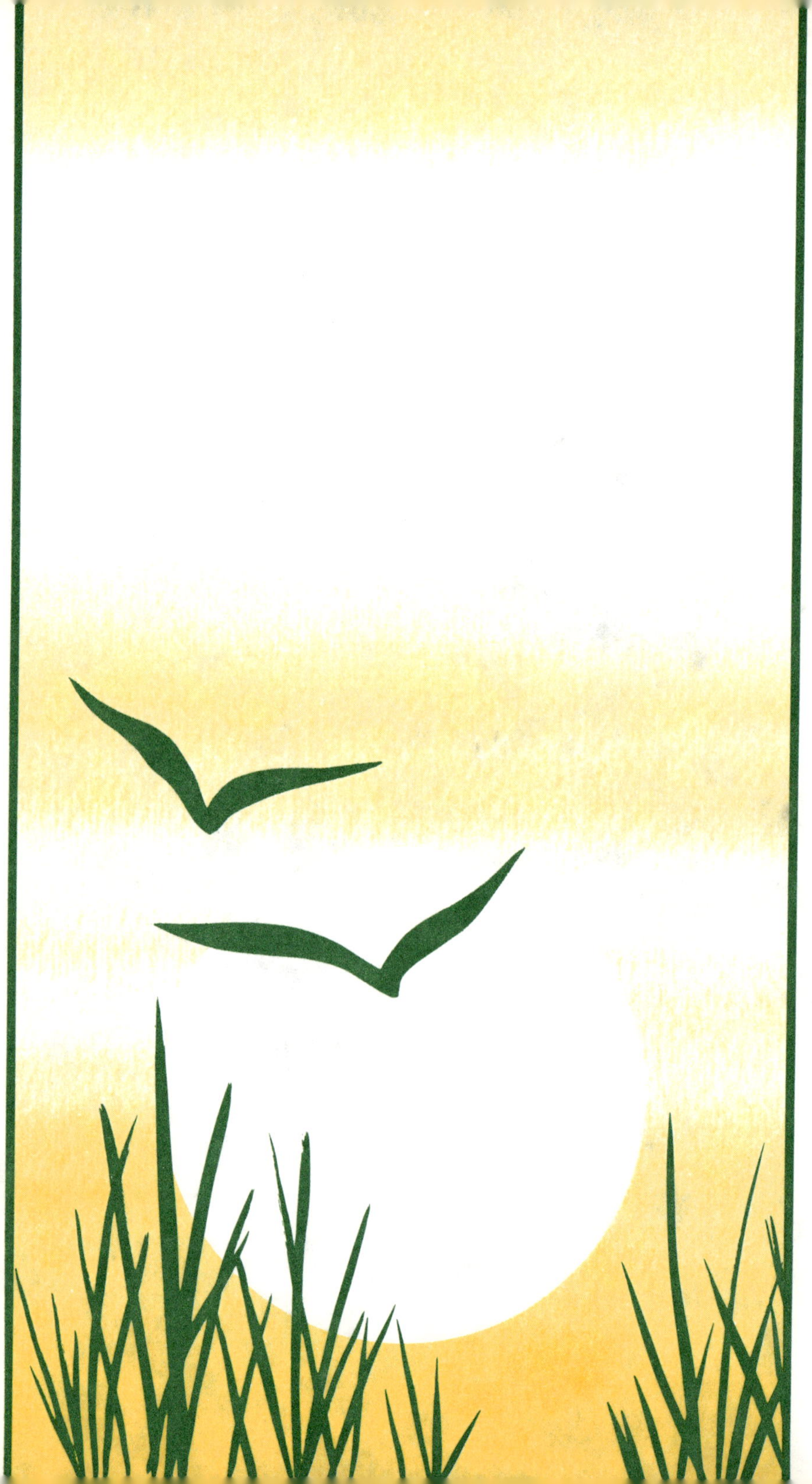

*I am
locked
within
myself.*

*A handful
of people
on this
earth
hold the
key.*

*You are
  one
of them.*

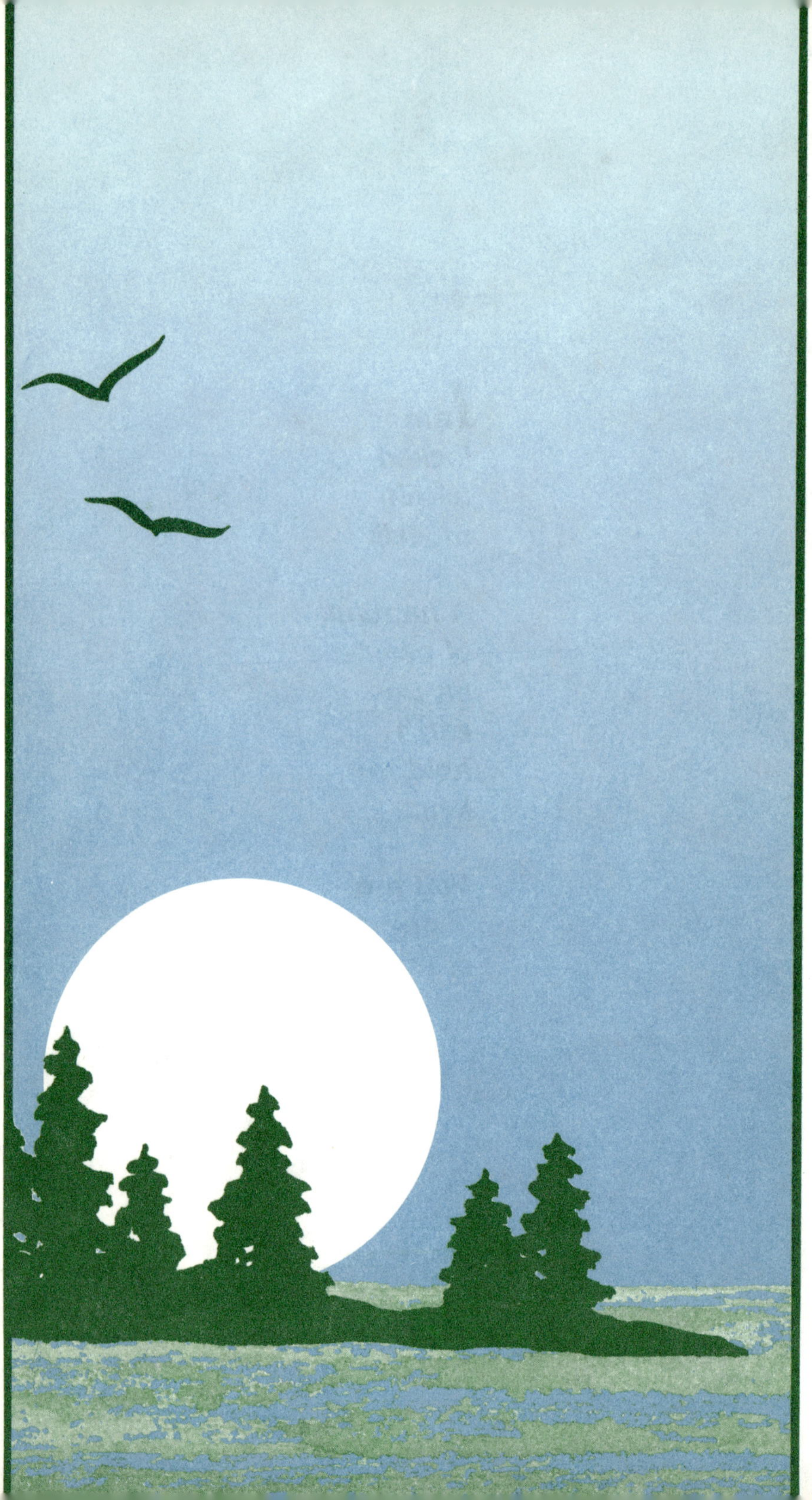

*We are such
good friends
you & I.

After being
with you
for only
a little while

I
no longer
relate to
sadness.*

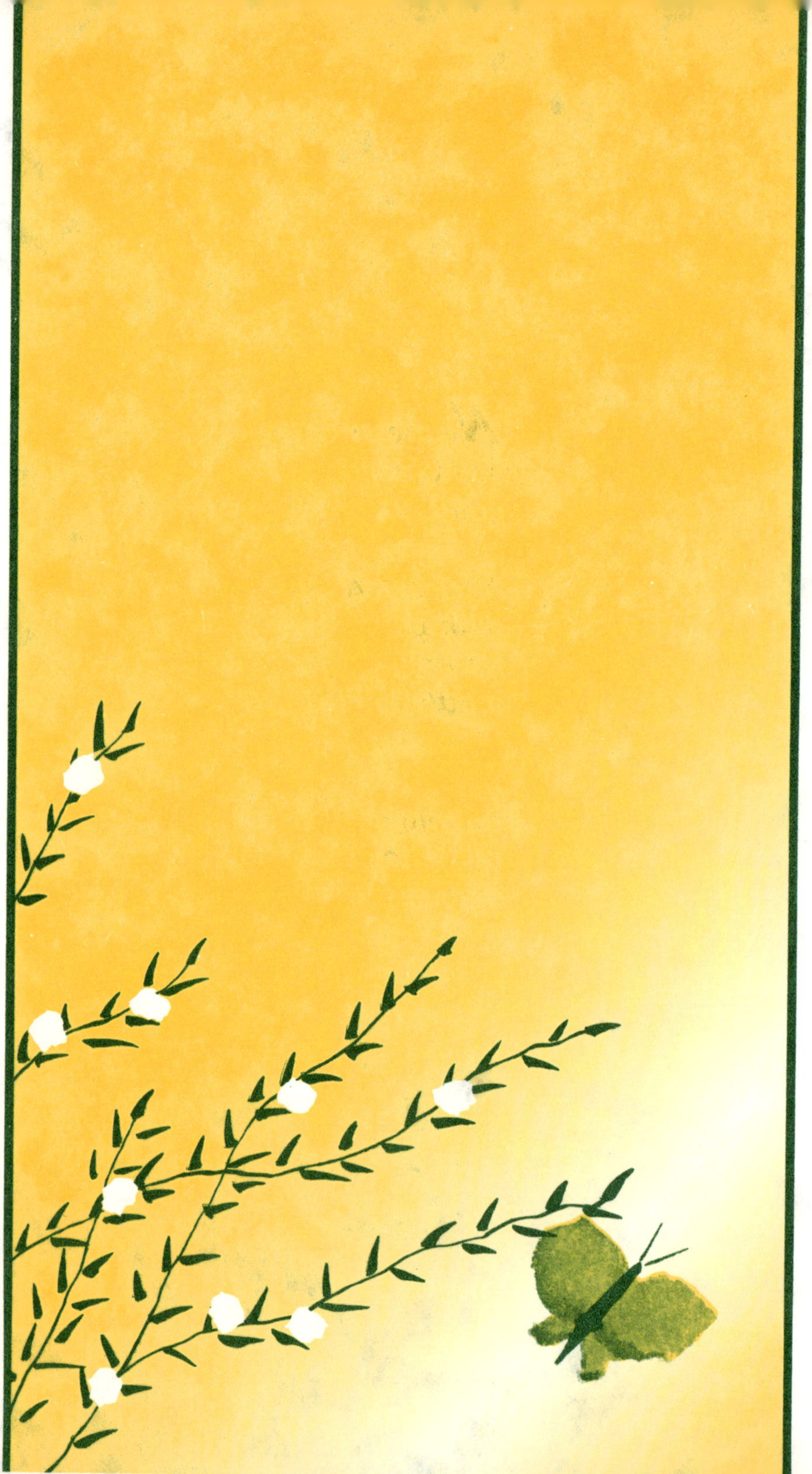

All I know is that

I love you.
I want you
Some times I need you.

You are someone
and being with you
something I
long for.

and I love you.

That's all I know

Acknowledgments:

Many of the poems that are included in this book
were previously copyrighted, and have appeared
earlier in the following books by Peter A. McWilliams:
Come to My Senses
For Lovers and No Others
I Love Therefore I Am
Love . . . an Experience of
Come Love with Me and Be My Life
The Hard Stuff: Love
Love is Yes
This Longing May Shorten My Life
Love and All the Other Verbs of Life
Evolving at the Speed of Love
Information about these titles is available through
Leo Press, 5806 Elizabeth Court, Allen Park, Michigan 48101

Any comments or questions about this book are welcomed
and can be sent to: Peter A. McWilliams, c/o Blue Mountain Arts, Inc.,
P.O. Box 1007, Boulder, CO 80306